# POETRY FOR…



To

Carol with love,

From your friend,

OB & Author
Michael

Michael Senteza Bagampangye

## Table of Contents

# Introduction

*Poetry for the Soul* is a collection of poems mainly written during the Covid-19 Lockdown. The poems are from a number of topics ranging from love, passion, success, compassion, desire, topics, politics, nature, connection, belief, commitment, childhood, seasons, courage, discovery, respect, dreams, weather, happiness, hunting, hope, identity, jealousy, Pucker, repentance, truth and endurance amongst many other topics that can not all be listed here.

Some of the poems cover different perspectives individuals might have about a particular topic and their possible reactions.

If you have a passion for poetry, reading, writing, and the interplay of words in the English Language, then try *Poetry for the Soul* with the "Poetic Musings straight from the heart" in the collection. You won't regret it.

## Animals

They come in twos domestic and wild

Both heterogeneous and homogeneous

What determines them is their character

Lions rule the jungles or the savannas

Cougars are sharp, feminine and strong

Lambs and Turkeys are victims

Cats and dogs are cuddly and cute

Parrots are noisy, while hamsters are prickly

Beavers, yes, beavers are a little dirty

Bears are wild and are said to be left-handed

Yes, it is about character

Snakes crawl and bite

Foxes are clever and determined

Rhinos are aggressive and strong

Hippos and crocodiles swim

Some are good, while others are bad… Cliche

But at the end of the day, Man is the most dangerous of these Animals

He also rules, controls and destroys

For future survival, man's control and aggression must be curbed

For through living as one with nature and other animals, man will have contributed much

For there is an animal in all of us.

## Atmosphere Universe Ocean and Seas

We are all in one and one in all

So one and all think about that atmosphere

The air we breathe in, the things we do, and the way we make others feel

It's all part of who we are

Not only who we are but who we could be as beings in the universe

We are part of the whole, and the whole is a collection of its members

We are as big as our team, and the team is as big as the individuals in it

Rolling in the deep, we all are

Who made all this? Is it the big bang theory or the biblical creation by the high and mighty in Eden?

Who are we, and what are our roles in this precarious and fragile realm?

What separates us is what connects us in the end

We are part of one whole drama moving on towards infinity and beyond

Turning in that proverbial widening gyre

Like a labyrinth it may seem, but the connection cannot be denied

Oceans, seas, rivers, lakes, mountains, the skies with those clouds and their silver linings, we are part of a whole, and the whole is a collection of us

Let's create a conducive atmosphere to help the universe

Let's make our humble contribution towards making the universe habitable for all

And maybe in our little way, this insignificant earth, this confusing realm, shall be heralded as a place where the universe was made better and more habitable for all using the given atmosphere and tools

Let us think big, for it's through those big thoughts that we can figure out who we could possibly be

After all, we are spirits in our current bodies travelling through the universe towards a destiny unknown

Let us do what we can where we are with what we have to contribute towards making a better universe.

## Bear Hug

Ever had that bear hag

Talk about connection

Nothing beats that human touch

One wonders, why the human touch is that endearing to one

As a man that is not afraid of being touched, or should I say one who craves that touch, I can surely say a human touch is such an enigma

The earliest I remember being touched is by my grandma while bathing and dressing me as a child. (NO, she didn't molest me). I felt an element of excitement that I have never found anywhere else

Even though I was not touched much, I found myself comfortable with bear hugs

When dad came from the city to occasionally visit, I always looked forward to those bear hugs

Fast forward to as an adult, human touch is one of my best experiences

One wonders, How about the other adult stuff? Well, I do not get that many of them nowadays. Maybe proper connection with that special one will knock cuddles off the patch as my top exciting touchy feelings

One wonders, are those bear hugs and the likes for kids? That would make me feel guilty of loving them, yet I am a grown man

What does one get from those bear hugs? What does one gain from them? Happiness, motivation, empathy, passion, and desire all come into play when one touches another human being

Although I came late to child television, watching Paddington bear fills me with excitement and joy and makes me a little passionate.

Now, brothers and sisters, for that matter, do not miss out on that personal touch, for that bear hug will give you that adrenaline rush that you cannot get from anywhere else

Go on, get that bear hug in there.

## Believed in me

You believed in me
Yes, You! You believed in me
Even when I thought I could not
You believed in me
As I was in the doldrums
You were there
Sometimes from a distance
And sometimes in person
You were there
Even in my doubt
You were there
Even in my worries
You believed in me
For now I worry
For disappointing you I worry
For my frustrations I worry
Yes I worry every day
You believed in me
So I should be
For you believed in me
For that reason I can live for you
For you believed in me my friend.

## Birds

They come in myriads number-wise

They come in myriads specie wise

Living in all corners of the earth

They are the pioneers of migration

Flying down south in winter and back north in spring and summer

avoiding the cold weather in the process

some scale the heights, while others do not fly

their species are uncountable

domesticated, some are,

Think of chickens, ducks, and of course, the delicious Christmas Turkey

Although some soar into the skies, they must Patch at one point or another

If one wants to be bad or free, they can soar as an Eagle

Excuse the imagery

The cowardly are called Chicken; the reason why, evades me

Peacocks hide in plain site

While so it is said, Pigeons are mothers of Journalism

Do not quote me, as this is off the record

Some are common; only in the great plains of Africa, the reason still eludes me.

Wild Geese in England and maybe other parts of Europe

Robins, Wrens and Kingfishers

In humanity, I am told, its slung for a beautiful woman

Flying and emigrating in numbers is a given for some of them

Some refer to it as a sign of freedom

Darwin Studied them first in the origin of species

His records and findings changed the world and the way we view them

They stand for many things: determination, flight, freedom, love making, mating, and more

You can be a bird regarding who you are, where you are, and what you think of yourself

At the end of the day, birds are an enigma

They have formed more than we know and have helped our civilisation, in many ways

In a way, they have formed the prototypes for flying objects like planes and drones

All said and done, birds soar, and so to be a bird, you need to be free to reach greater heights.

But please do not be a vulture.

## Chains

I am in chains
Yes, real chains
For loving you, I am
Loving you for one
Look!
I want them gone
All the chains and binds
Set me free
For my freedom is your freedom
Release me for I can
Yes, so I can let you go
For I have you freed
For my love is pure
Pure and true
Please undo these chains
For when I am free, you too will be free
For the love I have
You too can have
For the love I have, you too can have
Undo these chains, my love

## Childhood

For one to one it varies

But something is for sure: everyone has had one

Travelling through it takes you through a journey into the past, and what happens to you then, in most cases, determines how you end up as an adult, of course, apart from a few exceptional individuals.

Delving into my childhood, I see two different people coming into being. I see a young, impressionable man under the wings of his grandmother, loved, cared for but still troubled by queries about where his real parents were.

Delving deeper, I see a young man full of passion and desire but anxious about the world he lives in. Talk about a big head on young shoulders.

Everyone's childhood is different, but the most important needs by these said children are similar.

Children need happiness, freedom, nature and nurture, love, compassion, protection by adults, staying well-fed, warm clothing,

An early education for the child gives him or her a strong foundation to face this ever-precarious world at an advantage from an early age

Like it is said, what matters most is not what you leave for a child but what you leave in that said child

Childhoods are foundations for what one is to become later in life.

One would wonder, looking back, how did one's childhood determine who they become as adults?

How far back into your past do you recall? Do you have happy childhood memories? Do you genuinely feel that your childhood stood you in good stead to be the adult that you are now?

Did your childhood harness your creativity?

Looking back, how would you have wanted your childhood to be?

How would one transition from childhood to adulthood? What determines that said transition? Is it the physical or the mental transition that determines one so?

Did you enjoy your childhood, or did you hate it? What memories do you have from it?

Do you miss your childhood? Do you still have the child in you as an adult?

What did you get from your childhood that you would gift to the modern world or the child of today?

For after all, there is an inner child in almost all of us!!

Explore the child in you!

## Colours of Autumn

Seasons come and go
So it is a given that autumn does
Round the corner from summer
Close to winter and beyond
Seasons come and go and so does time
Leaves drop from the branches
The weather gets chilly and the atmosphere gloomy
In Charles' land and a few other places, even time changes
Seasons come and go as it is the eve of an ending year
One wonders, is autumn offering the best?
Yes the limited humidity and warmth
Of course warmer than winter
Some call it the end and others the beginning
Should we miss the summer or look forward to winter?
Snuggling on the sofa and sitting by the fire places come into play
Seasons come and go, and so do the bright summer days

The moods of the masses seem to darken like the days.
Late daylight in the morning and early darkness in the evening
Seasons come and go and so does life

Autumn is no end of life but the beginning of something new and special

Autumn brings beauty and prospects

Yes, prospects of a new era

And we reminisce the year almost gone

Seasons come and go, and so does autumn, with its colours and beauty

After all, seasons come just like the chill in the air

Just like heard over and over in my rhetoric

Seasons come and go

Gone is autumn and its colours, and we shall then wait

Yes, wait for another ten months before autumn with its colours come again

For indeed, autumn comes and goes just like all seasons

Those are colours of autumn

## Compassion

It's about understanding our differences and caring every day.

It's about knowing that they have their flaws and still care anyway.

It's about caring regardless of the circumstances.

It's knowing that we are all not perfect

It's about knowing that he or she just needs a little chat, a gentle touch or maybe a genuine smile.

Compassion is about having empathy even if they were not that good to you.

It's about simple acts of kindness even when they have not been good to you.

It's about finding that middle ground regardless of the circumstances.

It's knowing that they are not the best but care anyway

It's knowing that there must be something that makes them tick even in diverse circumstances.

It's showing them that they are loved, cared for and cherished even when they don't expect or deserve it.

Compassion is about loving, serving and being

It's about knowing what makes one tick and nurturing that.

So look into yourself and think, was I compassionate towards him or her? Could I do better or maybe serve them better than I did before?

Ask yourself, how much more compassionate can I be and then go do that, do that again, do more of that and then do better.

With compassion, you can win hearts and maybe win soul too.

## Conquering

We could conquer it all
Yes, the unforgetting elephant
The spying rat
The using fox
All in their boxes.
The running and freeing
Yeah, rhinos and all
They all seem to play all
Bold in their ways
Where does that leave you?
In doldrums sometimes
Dream within reach
Winning Probable
One has got to
Yes
To keep going
Destiny awaits
All you gotta do is
Keep going
Adios!

## Courage

It is the state of mind
The I can do attitude
It is both in nature and in nurture
It is about the desired goal
The end is improbable and intriguingly worth it in the end
It is for love and passion
It is about flying or actually jumping off a plane
Maybe jumping off that inflatable balloon
About that bungee Jump
Yes that Bungee jump off the falls

Scary it might be. But the feeling after? Irreplaceable
It is about motivation
The courageous do it; the cowards dread it
About worrying what he or she might do
What could possibly go wrong?
Why do you do it? What results do you want to achieve?
Motivation is key, indeed it is about love.
It's for the desire
It is about reaching greater heights
It's about discovering the improbable
Or previously unattainable

Your passion takes you there

Your nay Sayers say you can not

The variant say anything can happen

That ride on the rollercoaster

Parachute jumping? The boy racer in a banger!

Teenagers cycling

Talking to a stranger in a bar or at the bus stop

Approaching that lady or boy you always secretly desired

Travelling to new territories or horizons,

Penning that book you always wanted to

Spurring in that cage or boxing ring

Spurring with black belts in the dojo

Running that marathon

Telling a friend how you genuinely feel about them

Joining the forces, that tour of duty

Leaving home for new challenges and experiences

Taking that course, visiting that city or national park

Penning that movie, play or drama

Climbing Mount Everest

It's all hidden in there, make that speech

For yes, that is all courage

It comes in different shapes and forms

Determining of what it is is upon you

For courage comes dressed in different attires and forms

Go on, Brother or Sister, do take heart

Take courage, for the results after are insurmountable

Take that step

Take courage, my friend.

## New Day

At cock crow you know, Yesterday is gone
Today is here and tomorrow probably beacons!
For the end is a beginning of something new
Yes, the newness of life
Still yearning for an end, the cock crows at dawn

As I look through my history, memory floods in
It floods in like the Nile River on the African plains and dunes
Maybe I am on the right track
The car builders down south know
Yeah, the yearning and all
About my unknown history
My unknown destiny
Tricky but possible, enjoying the present moment.

Weep no more sad fountains
After the third time cock crow
Messiah looked at Simon
The disciple discovered for the betrayal was real
Seek, and you shall find
Ask, and it shall be given

Love, and you will be loved

The carmakers know it shall be a hunch

Do not forget the Ps and Ts (Please & Thank you)

## Discovery

The trap is set, the desire matchless
On the pillar of fame, discipline yourself
Search further, for the trek is long
On the Arabian Dunes, sub-Saharan Savannas
The European monuments and concrete Jungles
The Latin American Amazon Jungles
The large Oceans
The Ugandan gorillas
Birds Chapping in the trees, The Safari parks

Yes, the hunt is on, the search is on
Googling and Safari?
Yahoo and all the webs
The light bulb moments, the internet
All in one bound
And of course, life itself, we are at it
Yes, it is the real deal, it happens all the time
It is indeed... discovery.

## Disrespect

I listened to a little word that has caused more evil than good

The word is disrespect

They say respect takes ages to earn but a moment to be lost

For one has nothing to lose giving the said respect, but mankind tends to disrespect more than respect

Disrespect can cause heartache and pain and maybe cause hatred between individuals

I have seen racial tension caused by disrespect

Disrespect and stigma seem to come hand in glove

Reasons for disrespecting one another come in myriads

It could be envy, skin colour, sexual orientation, where one is from, age, sexuality, physical features, economic class, the kind of people one hangs with, academic achievements, one's job, what one owns and how one speaks, amongst many other pointers.

One would wonder why possession would determine one's level of respect

For if one drives a Lamborghini, Tesla, BMW, Jaguar, Bugatti or Mercedes Benz, the journey the car takes is the same as one driving a Toyota, Volvo, Hyundai, Honda or Ford. So why disrespect one because of their possession or lack of it?

Many wars, including two World Wars, have been fought because of the idea of disrespect.

If you want to get into any human being's bad books, show him or her disrespect. For we know that disrespect causes more trouble than it solves problems, then why do we still disrespect one another

Maybe it is because of humanity's brutish nature

Some people go a long way trying to earn respect even by doing things that should not be done, even ending up committing murder

For now that we know the evils of disrespect, why don't we try not to go disrespecting one another

Now that we know that disrespect causes more problems than it solves, why don't we respect each other more

For we know in more ways than one, respect is reciprocated, and so is disrespect to one another

Loving and respecting others is a virtue.

For at the end of the day, disrespect causes more harm than good, and it causes more problems than it solves.

Let us respect one another, for its then that we can create a better world.

## Distraction

Come hold my hand so I can show you an idea about Interruption

Come on now, so I can show you an idea of Disruption

Come see commotion take hold or maybe find a way of stopping it

Come closer and see Disturbance in another angle

Come and see us take that Diversion

Come get entertained from a different Angle

Come get diverted to your pass time that some call a Hobby

Come let us use that pass time in this Pass time that they call poetry

Come let us take a break, step hard on that brake lest we break

Come take a Pause, think hard, think

Come now take a kit kat that some call a Stoppage or a sabbatical

It is about Intrusion but brother, take heart only the sky is the limit

It is about taking that interlude from a great drama or musical show

It is about Intermission or probably Interference

It is about hitting hard when only being strong is all you have left in times of trouble

It is about fighting through the tumultuous situation or turmoil itself.

It is about staying strong in the middle of Uproar

It is about diverting your attention to Amusement or Recreation or probably controlling Activity

It is about Change from that that occupies you

Bear with me as we talk about Invasion, for our instruction is, let us not destroy

Let us not Fracture, Crash, meddle, disseminate, or cause harm, for if you live by the sword, you die by that sword

Let us look after mother earth, each other, younger generations of people, the less privileged or just pray for them if you cannot help them directly.

Let us have some empathy and love for one another or maybe just serve one another in our small way.

Let's reduce the anger and Annoyance if we can,

Let us walk in our brother's shoes for a mile before we judge them

Let's remove the clog in our eyes before we judge others or try to remove that that is in their eyes.

Let us avoid the hullabaloo but work to stop destruction and distraction, for that matter

For at the end of the day, destruction leads to distraction and all.

For destruction serves no one in the end.

**Dream**

Dream, Dream
Dream my friend
For if you dream, something will
Something will come of it
Dare to dream
Dare to dream it all
Dare!
After all you can
When you wake up for...
The dream will still stand
Will stand like a tower
Taller than the Shad
Taller than the BT Tower
Taller than the Eiffel Tower
Towering over the mountains
For when you dare to dream
Anything could happen.
For I do dream and envision
I envision what could happen if
Yes if..
If I dared to dream
For the stuff of dreams is

Is soup for the soul and all

## Element

It could be a state of mind or thought process

It is maybe about the feeling inside

Or that chemical reaction that science tends to bring forth

One thing is for sure, whatever the element efficacy comes into play

Maybe it is about earth, water, wind or fire

Watching the Last Air Bender. Yeah a movie about the elements

The power of Martial Arts in bending the air in the 21st Century comes into play

Martial Arts is maybe the fifth Element after the major four

How does desire come into play when talking about the elements?

For achieving the elements: Chemical or not, desire is paramount!

How does one relate desire to the elements?

Maybe it is about nature and nurture!

After all, to harness the elements, the best way is to go for what you strongly desire and work towards it with all your might!

In doing so, you will be closer to conquering the elements!

Element can also be a state of being!

Yeah, being in your element can stand for how you are in the moment. Time comes into play!

Yes, the moment in the trajectory of time and energy is part of the element

One would wonder, how is it possible to conquer the elements?

Maybe, as they say, anything is a possibility!

So there!! Conquering the element is an elementally object worth trying for!

So there. Whatever the element, whatever the desire, strive to conquer the elements, and you will indeed be in your element!

It is just elementally!!

**Endurance**

It comes in different forms

Dressed in different ways and means

What it is to Tom is not exactly what it is for Dick and Harry

What it is for Jack isn't exactly what it is for Jill.

It could be going through the maze

It could be through the labyrinth

It could be Turning and turning into the gyre like one poet famously mused

Maybe it is swimming in the Thames

Maybe swimming down the river Nile snaking across Africa

Maybe swimming down the Mississippi

Maybe along the Kazinga channel connecting Edward to George

Always swimming against the tide

Sink or swim is the order of the day

Could be finishing that degree even if you have been diagnosed mentally ill.

Could be keeping going when the world seems to isolate you and leave you in limbo

Could be running a marathon like a Kenyan, Ethiopian or Ugandan

Yes, Ugandans are good at it too

Forget Mo Farah, this is the real deal.

Could be an African child walking five kilometres to collect water or firewood

Could be a five-kilometre barefooted walk to school along the Sahara Dunes, or the African plains

Could be a scotching heat walk to an oasis in the Arabian deserts

Could be going hungry for days, saving the only food for the young ones

Could be bees building a colony, or ants searching for food and shelter

Could be an adventure trek to Mount Everest's peak

Could be that eye on a beautiful girl in the neighbourhood

Could be a test of one's mental agility to handle it all

Maybe finishing that book you are penning

Finishing Scripting that movie

Protecting your bread and butter

Beating those deadlines

Spurring with another black belt

Waiting for your one opportunity of a lifetime

Its survival for the fittest

Staying in that relationship for the sake of your kids

Keeping in that job for the sake of making ends meet

Getting on that podium to make that speech even when you do not know what to say

Maybe it's surviving that lockdown or two

Endurance comes dressed in different forms

Endurance makes the result sweeter

Endurance makes the win worthwhile

Endurance is working towards obtaining those seemingly unattainable goals.

Endurance is keeping going even when the odds seem stacked against you.

Endure.

## For I believe in you

Yes you!
For the belief is real
It's all about me and you
For it's the two of us
Sailing through it all
For it's that that matters
For I do care about you!
How to prove so
For I don't know
But that still stands
For the belief is true
For you toiled with me
And I toiled with you!
Yes! The belief is real
Where we are going
Nobody knows!
We are still hand in hand
The journey is ours.
Yes, you and me
Destination
Nobody knows
But sill we shall go

Embark on the journey

With faith we shall!

## Friday the 13$^{th}$

It is the ying and the yang

It is either evil or Angelic

Probably satanic or spiritual

It could be a day like any other

Just another day on a calendar

Myriads love it

And in the same veil Myriads hate it

Why hinge all your bets on just a day

There are 365 days or maybe 366 annually

Just one or two fall on the day

Think

Why attach so much meaning onto a single day?

What is the difference between this and other days in the year?

Where did it originate?

Why is it so important to so many?

Why do people nurture its idea?

What would they aim to achieve?

Does the high and mighty know about it?
After all, He is said to be all-knowing.

All knowing? Really? Seriously?

That could be Magical or scientific

Let's digress, how is that possible?

All-Knowing!!!

Who could know it all?

Is it an algorism?

Is it quantum?

What is the paradigm?

Could this day really have a major meaning?

Love it or loath it, Friday the 13th is up there amongst those days and beyond

Special or not, Friday the 13th is a day to reckon.

## Fur

Treading through my little neck in the woods, I think of my furry friend

I got thinking about fur and all its trappings

Does the fur protect one from the heat during summer, or does it keep one warm during winter?

Fur to carpet makers is gold dust and so it still is to cloth makers

Watching a farmer sheer the sheep on television, one light bulb moment jumps into my mind, how did the high and mighty create the multi-faceted creatures that not only give fur but can be a delicious component of a stew?

That is just lamb or goat. Please do not make stew out of some other fury friends like cats and dogs.

Does it occur to you when you sit on that carpet, or when you wear that woollen attire the time, money and energy used to get to it?

Look after your furry friends, and they will look after you for a good turn deserves another.

For there is always a way to wear fur, and the finest fur may cover the toughest meat

And others say they may rather go naked than wear fur, you have your own opinion

For the choice of how you relate to or use fur is a personal thing

Go on think about and look at fur in a different and unique way.

## Glass

Is it about a glass ceiling?

Or it is about a glass half full or half empty

How does one break that glass ceiling?

Should it be by force or by compromise?

How does one break the glass? Maybe it's a singer's note that can literary break the glass.

But throwing it down is the easier way to break the proverbial glass.

Maybe it is that glass of wine on a Friday evening. For we are all mortal until the first kiss and maybe the second glass of wine

One wonders where does glass come from?

How is glass made? Who discovered it? And when was it discovered?

Should a person trouble himself with where the glass came from?

Looking through one's spyglass let us talk SIS, Mi5, FBI, CIA, MOSSAD, KGB, GESTAPO or maybe the little-known CMI

Why is glass important in one's being? For broken glass is like glitter, it is all dependant on how you view it

Maybe it is because of the various products glass can make. Or is it about a philosopher who can look at an empty glass with a smile.

Cups, vases, drinking glasses, bottles, plates, mirrors, decorations or pint glass

Maybe it is the looking glass, spectacles, or shades, or sunglasses

Could it be a window or door glass?

Or maybe we could go satirical for it's through satire that a glass where beholders do generally see everybody's face but their own

## Glass 2

It is the pros and cons, yes, Ying and yang
Back and forth, top to bottom, or bottom upwards
Tos and fros, start to end
Genesis to revelations
Beginning to end
A few huddles prevail
Challenges prevail, a few knocks
Yes few or many.. knocks
They will be met along the way

Yes it is the mean, the real centre
The intersection of the Ven diagram
Could be the centre of the Universe
Half way through the Journey,
The space between the beginning and the end
The seed to the fruit
In humanity, it is Mulato

For machines, it's Turbo or Hybrid
In the ages, it is probably the middle Ages.
Say I can win or I cannot win. In both ways, you are right
Your state of mind is yours to control

For life happens to you or for you

It is all in the mind.

For you have the glass in your hands

For it is for you to know if

If it is half-full or half-empty

## Happiness

Enigmatic it is, but one would say, it is a state of mind
Who determines what it is?
In your heart of hearts, what is it to you?
What makes you think you are in that state?
What would it take for you to be so?
What determines if you are?
Are you in charge of it yourself?

Is it a stroll on the beach?
Is it a walk in the park?
A sense of contentment?
What do you have to achieve or be to think you are it that state?
Is it a workout in the gym?
Spurring with another talented fighter?
A friendly pat on the shoulder?
A shot in the arm?
Seeing someone you love
Seeing someone you have not seen for a while

Maybe it is about winning something
Maybe it is a trophy in the debating club?

Maybe it is your team winning a crucial match.

Maybe it is your young one achieving something monumental

Maybe it is cuddling up with someone you really and genuinely like

Maybe it is visiting a fantastic place you have never been before

Maybe it's revisiting a place close to your heart.

Maybe it is making love to someone you truly love or one you are connected to

Maybe it is making that inspiring speech on the podium

Maybe it is a feeling of genuine contentment after achieving a milestone

Could it be because of a compliment you just received?

Could it be a smile from a stranger? How precious

Could it be after solving or working out something complex?

Could it be just after listening to your favourite song on the Radio?

Could it be watching your favourite movie?

Could it be getting that position, promotion or being hired for a great role?

Could it be inspiring your team to that great win?

Could it be after winning that contract?

Could it be after hitting that deadline

Tell me friend

What is it to you?

Where do you find yours?

Tell me friend

Whom do you find it in?

Tell me friend

Do you ever make someone so?

Tell me

How many people have you inspired to feel so?

Tell me

How can we make the masses feel so?

Tell me friend

Are you passionate about it?

For all said and done, no one determines your happiness; you can only find it inside of you.

It is indeed a personal state of mind.

Find your happiness.

## Hunting.

He was out there

Out there hunting

Whatever for, nobody knew

Was it something new?

Who did what where?

Did he love them?

Or did they love him?

What could he do with it?

With what where?

With the love to them all

Did he have love in his heart?

Yeah! In his heart of hearts

For I know.

After all, it was all about him

Or so he thought.

## Hope

It is a battle

Yes I mentioned the B word

It is a battle between optimism and pessimism

It's about seeing a possibility in every problem other than seeing a problem in every possibility

It's about hoping for the best even when faced with adversity

It's about always seeing that proverbial light at the end of the tunnel

It's about seeing that silver lining in every cloud

It's about falling down seven times and getting up eight times

It's about knowing in your heart of hearts that things will get better in one way or another

It's about loving that seemingly unlovable lady or man, for that matter

It's that love for one, regardless of those flaws in them

It's about looking into yourself and imagining what you could possibly become

It's leaving your country for foreign lands, not knowing what the new country has to offer

It is the patience of waiting for that take away after ordering and paying online or by phone.

Could be Posting a letter and waiting for a reply from the subject

Could be knowing that one day you will get out of poverty, not knowing the hows and whens

Could be assuming things will get better even when diagnosed with a chronic illness

Talk of that schizophrenia or cancer

Could be taking that proverbial first step of a thousand miles

Must be going where there is no path and leaving a trail

It is about doing what you can where you are with what you have

Must be believing that no matter how hard of how tough it gets, I am going to make it.

It is about not believing that things are always going to be the way they are,

It is about changing and working while believing in the best of possibilities

Must be going boldly where no man has ever been before

Must be knowing that you will get there even when you do not know how

Must be believing in that Alfa and Omega even without any proof

That belief in the ever-all-knowing Deity

After all, blessed are those who believe without seeing

It is about not thinking why me and going try me

It's knowing that the harder the battle the sweeter the victory

Success might be slow but through hope and patience, hope is for the best

Hope, Hope, Hope

Hope is working and going towards your desires just armed with belief

Nothing is impossible if you work and you are armed with hope

For it is the hopeful and optimistic that will conquer the world

Hope often perpetuates existence.

## Ordinary Man

I am an ordinary man
I live and ordinary life
In an ordinary land
The query lingers
What's ordinary
What's extra ordinary
Maybe I put my cornerstone
And a brother puts another one
For slowly by slowly
One day we shall get there
Wherever that is
Nobody knows
Actually probably He
Yeah He knows!
For He is not of our ways
He is an extraordinary one.
An extraordinary man
Maybe we should just praise him.
After all, millions
Yes, millions and generations
Have done so too
After all its

Always about him

## I Can See You

I can see you

Yes I can see you.

You are at the centre of it all, my love

You are beautiful

You are well-bodied

You are humble

Funny

Yes you are funny to

You are between them

You are all and one

My love is for you

For you and them

For you are Sapphire

Probably Nefertiti

For you are

You are true and all

I beg no more of you,

But your true self

Is it true love or is it lust?

Whatever it is

It was a lesson and all

It taught love

Taught me to love
Love for the sake of it all.
For the sake of love
I could say I love you
But for now, I can say
You are one of a kind
Come on, let's live and love.
For they say
Love conquers all.

**Love hate:**

I hate to love you so much
I love to hate your ego
Your game heightens my determination
Not to conquer you for now
But for the life there after
To control and own your strings
Attaching them to my soul
Then driving you to the edge
Not with pain but with passion
To conquer your soul
To take it with me
On my journey across the universe
Praying to the maker- to
Dissolve the differences
Show the similarities
For I know you
I know your soul
I know your will
I know your power
But make no mistake, we are two of a kind.
You look into me as I look into you.
You could have driven me insane

But that is me already.

You could have made me cry

But my tears shade for all mankind.

You could have made me want you more

But I already want you enough.

Now jump off that horse that you cuddle so much

Disentangle yourself from the cuddle with that dog

Let me hold you

Let me take you onto a journey unknown

For when we get there,

it will be me and you,

Now and forever

For you are indeed

Queen.

## Identify

Point one out from the crowd

Give one a name or call them for what they are known

Follow through to find what makes them tick

Who are you? What are you? Who do you think you are?

Where are you from?

How do you view who you are?

What makes you tick?

Who would you fall for?

Is it about gender? Ethnic background or sexuality?

Is it about one's position in society?

Think about class system

Or maybe where and what you studied?

Or is it about which part of the town you live in?

Or maybe what your parents did for a living?

What do you stand for and what are your values?

What are your aspirations, desires, and goals?

What have you achieved as an individual?

What are your personal accomplishments?

Tell me your friend, and I will tell you who you are.

What do you do and whom do you do it with?

Where do you like going?

Birds of the same feathers flock together, which other birds do you flock with?

Are you that bird in the first instance?

What are your favourite hobbies and pastimes?

Do your desires come into play when thinking of who you hang out with or what keeps you busy?

What sort of books do you read?

What is your favourite restaurant or Cafe?

Who are you my friend?

Do you even know who exactly you are?

What makes you think you are who you think you are?

What makes you think you are who you think they think you are?

What makes you think?

Do you think in the first instance?

What makes you think you do think?

And what does make you think that what you think matters?

How do you impart your information into society?

Is that part of your identity?

How do you identify yourself?

Could that be exactly who you are or what you assume you are?

Who determines who you are in the first instance?

At the end of the day, you identify yourself as who you are and nobody can decide your identity for you.

You are who you are my friend, and that's how you should identify yourself.

No body, I repeat, nobody can decide the way you identify yourself

Your identity is Personal to you.

## Jealousy

A dangerous disease eats humankind up

The disease that has no cure

The disease whose origin is unknown

But I tell you friend avoid that killer disease

For if you fall prey to it, your life will never be the same.. But in a negative way

It kills like a cancer and the danger is it kills the individual not that one that they are jealous of

Jealousy is a killer, it comes slowly and keeps creeping up slowly by slowly

Jealousy is a killer indeed, it drives you into a rage like nothing else

I know they say that we sometimes believe that the grass is greener in the neighbour's lawn

This could ring true sometimes, but we sometimes pay too much attention to that said neighbour's lawn and forget to see the good in our own lawn

There is a disease my friend, it kills destroys, and annihilates more than a double-edged sword

A disease that has no cure other than kill, destroy and eradicate like a plague

There is a disease my friend, a disease whose origin is unknown, but pray it goes back where it's from

This disease kills slower but steadily than we could widely believe or imagine

The major danger is that this Jealousy disease kills the bearer other than that that the jealousy is directed to.

There is a disease that works like a boomerang, you toss it out and it comes back to you

Talk about self-harm, this jealousy disease hurts the barer than the subject of the jealous themselves

One wonders where it comes from but some say low self-esteem and poor self-image comes into play when thinking about where it is from

My friend stand guard at the gate of your mind and do not let jealousy creep up on you for remember

Yes, remember feelings are not facts!

And jealousy destroys none other than the jealous themselves

## Journey

It is 1000 Miles, take step one

Whichever boots you wear

From Cradle to grave, yeah, birth to death

From January to December

From Dusk to dawn or dawn to dusk

From Morning to evening

From Childhood to Adulthood

From point A to point Z

From number one to infinity

It is indeed a widening gyre

Crawl, Walk, run, Cycle, ride, drive, or fly

The choice is yours

To infinity and beyond

Brother don't crawl, for it will take forever

Swim or sail even against the tide

For it is a race, run your own

Shoot for the sky

For if you miss, at least you will be amongst the stars

For when you reach, reach out and pull one up

Yes, pull a brother or sister up

For its those small acts of kindness that matter at the end of the day

Go all the way to the end

When you get there understand

Understand that that is just the beginning

It is the beginning and the new journey awaits.

## Maze

Jump into the Maze of life
Join in with the mystery souls
Think.
About what you could be
Oh maybe, maybe
What you could have been
Think again. Think
About cleansing the soul
Yes, the soul and all.
Dominate
Not only your peers
But your fears too!
Unite, with
Not only your mate
But with your pet
Not only with your pet
But with your inner might
Jump, not to touch the ceiling
But to catch the fleeing.
CATCH?
Oh yeah Catch
The sky and the stars

Overtake

The leader in the race.

Win, not wine

Dine, not fine

Help not haunt

And remember

We all are in the maze!!

## Know Love

One day you will know

Yes you will.

You will know that I did

For I did love you

Past? Why not the present?

What is in the present?

Could I have one?

Could I give what I can?

How much does it cost?

The yen could do but I choose love

The Rand could do but I moved continents

How about that Shilling?

Is it enough for them all?

What did they do for it?

For nobody knows

And you would wonder

What does she get out of it?

Possibly love

Yes, love and its trappings

For them it will ...

It will be worth the wait

Yes my friend

Know Love. For it conquers all.

## Life Through the Lens

At your vantage point you see it clearly
It could be a dream, it could be a desire
It might be for love and probably lust
Tom's view is good but different from Harry's
Harry's view is different from Dick's but Dick's view is valid to
As you set off onto your Journey
The dreamer in us wonders, am I on the right track?
What is the right track anyway?
Who determines what that track is anyway?
Where is that track heading to?
Do I need the track, or should I go where there isn't one and I leave a trail?

What do I see for the future at my vantage point?
Is it achievable? How do I make it come forth?
How do I Reach for the heights?
How do I view my journey?
In whose perspective do I see that journey?
What steps am I taking to achieve it?
Is there a silent observer or its only my personal view?

Ask the what? Who? Why? How? and when?
For questioning puts things in perspective
It is only viewed through an individual's Lens.
It has come and gone
But that is just me, the romantic at heart
It could have been penned,
For my view is not exactly your view
It only depends on the viewer's vantage point
But in my view, life happens
Your opinion is your entitlement
As the man or Woman in the mirror
Your perspective matters,
After all, it is your life through the lens.

**Lockdown**

The rather impressionable child knew it

Even before he knew what it was.

Absence of evidence is not evidence of absence

In childhood, he never knew the meaning

After all, a child that never travelled thinks mum is the best cook

Even now he still thinks so.

With the childhood friend and rival he did it

Yes, a few times he did while fighting back

So he did in the subconscious mind, yeah, the inner continuum

And once to the school bully, he so did to

Fast forward in the dusty pothole-riddled Kampala street

While watching television shows from Europe and America

At the Muchomberos, the lovely Congolese neighbours

He watched it for the first time

Yes, on that little black-and-white television set

**Remember that?**

On the screen, he saw the likes

The Undertaker, Hulk Hogan, The Rock, Michael Hayes and many more

Yes, it was the WWF

He saw that strangle hold a few times

Cheering on he did as though he was part of those in the Arena

Yes the Madison Square Gardens

Twenty Years on in the paved London Concrete Jungle

Under tutorage of Gintas, the forces guy and master

Yeah, his new Sensei

In that little Gym in Watford,

He learnt further the military chokes and strangleholds

To save one's self all he needed was to tap out, Simply put

In the Troxy Arena in East London he watched

Yeah he watched his spurring mates at it

It's the famed Mixed Martial Arts (MMA). To be concise

Wait for it, **Lockdown**

If you cannot save yourself, Tap out

Come 2020, this word Lockdown had a new and different meaning

Listen Friend

Towards spring 2020, I am told there broke out a pandemic imported from the Far East

(Imported?) Haa Haa

A solution, simple-

Wash Hands, keep a safe distance, socially Distance or wear that proverbial mask

Alternatively socially isolate or quarantine like African long-horned cattle

Now the word has a new meaning, yeah still talking about Lockdown

Wonders never cease, How can one get in lockdown in isolation?

Anyhow anything is possible

So now we know,

Away from Martial Arts, there can be lockdown without contact

For almost two years, the whole world (Apart from Tanzania) was in contactless lockdown

## Love part Two

I do love you and beg of you
Please let me love you.
For you have always been
The love of my life
Not only lover but a friend to
For they say it conquers all
Let's conquer all with love
To you my friend I give the love
For you deserve it and more
Just for loving me
I will give you genuine love
And it will blow your mind
For now and ever
For I do love you my friend.

## Love

I could love you

Actually not could, but can

Yes you stole it

You stole my heart

For it was pure

It could be pure now

But then it's all beyond

Could you love me?

Just like, I love you!

Could you teach me how?

Yes, how to love you more

Yes, to love you more

For I still have some.

Yes! Some love to give.

For my heart is pure!

For we can love

Let's love each other

For it's you and I for now

To infinity and beyond

Better snatch it

Before someone grabs it

For its pure and fragile.

And the truth still stands,

For I love you my friend!

## Loving Theme

Loving them all
Pigeons and doves
Vultures and Eagles
I love them all
For they to belong
After all they all need
Yes need a home to go to
ram shackled and all
Dilly dallying yes
Where is the direction?
What does the future hold?
Both for me and for them?
What does the future hold?
For us and all.
Where does it leave us?
Does anyone know?
What should they know?
Why should they know?
For whom should they know?
Let's dream it all
Let's conquer it all
Since after all

All is one!

## Loving

To you my friend
They don't love you
So they pretend
They don't respect you
For they despise you
Speak they do
So they do behind your back
Yes my friend!
I mean you.
You my true friend
They just use you!
To my friend I thought
I would bring salvation
Can I do it alone?
No I can't.
Actually-yes, probably!
How will I save you?
Yes! You my friend
Ask and
And so it shall be given
Yes my dear friend
For I love and care about you

Let's do something

Yes, me and you!

Let's love one another!

For it conquers all!

## Walpurgis Night/May day

Christianity comes with its own perk

Celebrations come in bounds

Think of the birth of the servant king, Noel He is called

How about his death and resurrection, famously called Good Friday and Easter Sunday respectively

How about ascension (the day of Pentecost) when the servant king went back to the father

Come the end of April and beginning of May, we have the famous, actually the not-so-famous day

The day of feasting named after the famous saint Walpurgis

Dated back from the pagan celebrations of fertility and the coming of spring

Yes, spring has sprung and we are now to celebrate that mundane day

This day named after that German-English lady, talk about dual nationality

Humankind with his continuous excuse to celebrate could not let this day pass him by

As they celebrate Halloween end of October and early November, Walpurgis night comes as spring springs and now brings with it an excuse

Setting up Borne fires in Sweden Finland and other European countries mark the day

Intriguingly enough, it is associated with witches and yet it is a Christian celebration

As we look for excuses to celebrate, let's mark our calendars
this spring when witches ride to appointed rendezvous

It may come with its own nightmares, but this day, first
termed in 1823, is another reason to get out your party
poppers every mayday of every year

Happy Mayday or, concisely, happy Saint Walpurgis Day!
This spring.

## Mid-Winter Festival

It is the evening of the year
Gloomy dump and chilly
Hibernation is the order of the day
Day breaks late and night early
Wedged in between Autumn and spring
Sometimes snow, white like clean teeth
Kids and adults out with their sledges
Snowmen made, Clothes worn in layers and thick

Yes, it is holiday time
Loads of partying and dancing
Turkeys murdered in numbers
Potatoes baked, sweet sprouts cooked
Families from far and near come together
Presents under the Christmas tree in the living room
Work suspended for some and double pay for others
Did I mention Santa?

Look You!
The highlight of the season, His Birthday
Yes born in the manger our Christ
Star came from the east

To see that God-born man

The spiritual celebrate him

Pagans and atheists Loath him

Believers pray to and through him

Yes, it is the mid-winter festival

Time to make merry and show love

It is time for it all

Yes, it's the mid-winter festival

The time our lord was born

Make love and be merry.

## Ascend to the Top

Looking up from the foot of the mountain, one would think it is insurmountable

One wonders, is it possible to get to the top? After all, it is said anything is possible

What effort does one need to get to that said top?

Do they call it top or peak, pardon me for English is not my first language

Is climbing a mountain symbolism for a journey through life?

What would it take for one to get from the bottom to the top, (Should I say peak?)

It could be the Rwenzori, the Kilimanjaro or even the Everest

Whatever the mountain you need to climb, you better harness your ropes, for it will not be an easy feat

The climb is exhausting, tiresome, gruelling, demanding, difficult, tough or arduous, for luck of a better word

The climb up the mountain might not be forgiving, but the feeling when you get to the top of that said mountain is worth the effort taken to get through that taxing ascent

Maybe climbing a mountain is a metaphor for tackling a hard task. It is taxing, but the results are desirable, and looking down from the top, one realises the effort was worthwhile.

As an individual, you have your own Mountain to climb, it might take you a minute, hour, day, week, fortnight, month, year, decade or a lifetime. But getting to that peak is what matters at the end of the day.

It is about what you can achieve in the end, but don't forget to enjoy the process, for it is the main part to remember along the climb

The mountain you conquer is tailor-made for you personally, put a leg above the other and another leg above the other and repeat the same movement over and over, and in the end, you will be at the zenith.

When you get to the zenith, look back, lift an individual or two and help them harness their own journey to the top

And by doing so your climb will have been meaningful and your efforts and purpose will have made a mark onto this ever-precarious life.

Climb your mountain, and when you get to the top please don't leave your humility behind as you climb for you need it wherever you end up during and after the climb.

Now let us go and conquer that mountain!!

**An Overview About Love!**

Hear me, hear me out friend

Yes, keep your ears to the ground, or maybe keep your eyes peeled

Let us address the elephant in the room

Let's talk mental health. Are you mentally healthy, or do you suffer mentally?

Are you schizophrenic? Maybe you are depressed or autistic

Never mind. You are not alone!

Hear me, hear me out friend!

Ever heard of a narcissist? I am told he or she is the mentally ill

Forget the inner coiled or stressed!

Here we are talking about the mental disorder (or should I say the mental order)

It is about how you feel as an individual

I am told, pursuit of gratification is a mental disorder!

Some say it is from vanity or egotism!

Hear me, hear me out friend

It is about your self-image!

The Greeks tried it out centuries ago.

English writers tried it out too!

But Greek mythology claims one man fell in love with
himself and thus was called narcissistic!

With the modern-day mirrors and gadgets, maybe one can
fall in love with one's self!

Hear me hear me out my friend!

I would rather fall in love with a fair lady other than myself

It is a personal choice, So you rather hear me out friend!

Hear me out, hear me out my friend

Narcissus tried it once.

It is simple and clear, fall in love with someone or something
or maybe yourself!

There life will probably be worth living!

For what is the world without love?

I hear love makes the world go round after all!

Hear me, hear me out my friend

Love, Live, Be!

Hear me hear me out my friend

If it makes you Narcissist to Love, Live or Be then shoot!

Yes! Go for it, go love someone or yourself

If it makes you Narcissist, then let it be!

Go pursue your pleasure

But remember to do it with humility!

## New horizon

Achieving one goal is GETTING TO a particular horizon

For there is more to learn or achieve after achieving your first

One wonders where are the afore mentioned horizons

It can be anything from growing up?

Achieving a milestone, completing a task or beating a deadline

One wonders how many Horizons has one been through in their lifetime?

How long is a piece of string?

Or maybe is the glass half full or half empty

Personally I have been through a few horizons

Growing up, leaving my rural village in Mbarara moving to Kampala, Uganda's capital.

That to was a journey through new Horizons

Finishing Primary, secondary school and university was reaching new horizons to me

Travelling from Africa to Europe to me was new horizons Maybe reaching a new Horizon is reaching or achieving a particular goal

Finishing that book? A New Horizon!!

Going through the stringent British Immigration system to become a naturalised citizen could be another new Horizon

How about the work one does? Maybe monetising it would be another new horizon to go through

How do you get people to understand your input, making them go into new horizons?

How about we address the elephant in the room… yeah mental health.

How does one reach new horizons recovering from mental ill health?

Do people recover? What if you don't recover? Would that mean that you have not been to new horizons?

So brother, or sister, for that matter, what is a new horizon for you

Maybe when you get to that new horizon, look back, take a deep breath and think.

Phew, that was a bumpy ride

INDEED, that was a journey never to forget!!

A journey to the here and now, which is indeed a journey to new horizons!!

Reaching new Horizons is another chapter in this long precarious journey called life.

**Sasha's Dad!**

It started in the African Savannas,
The Luo Man chasing a dream,
Across the pond he went,
Seed sowing he did,
History was born- Officially
Today cemented
The indelible ink of He-
That dared to dream

A thousand miles is the journey
That solo step counts
The great robber may have taken
But their dream lives on
In the unhinged Dream
Born and raised rainbow
Reverie embedded in his soul
The journey improbable

LOOK ye sleeper
Meditate outside the box
Critic the self,
Task the inner Gods
Get in combat like a Viking
Not with his wrath but his mettle
Just like Sasha's (euphemism for Him)
The efficacious orator

Plain sailing it is not
Hills and valleys immense

Abraham started it
Malcolm X took the Barton
Brother Martin took the bend
And now-
Made of stuff of legend
A Powerful Man in a powerful land.

## State of Being (Pandemonium)

Let me take you on a mental trip a few years ago

I heard this English word for the first time on a book faire

I saw a male queen, yes, I mean a real male queen

He was so slim with the waist of a 16-year-old 15th Century English actress

Dressed all in white, with loads of makeup and high heels

A Beautiful necklaces glittering like real gold

Yeah, he or should I say she was dressed like a drag queen.

This reminds me of the dead or alive singer Pete.

Maybe I should talk about Boy George!

I had to research what that mouthful word meant

Maybe I heard it before two years ago but never took notice of it

Maybe the male queen's attire and look made me pay more attention to the word.

But still, it hasn't escaped my mind

It reminded me of the messy Taxi parks or shopping centres in my native Uganda

Ever wondered why when you see or hear something and pay attention to it for the first time it seems to be everywhere?

Probably, it is my mind in Pandemonium.

What does Pandemonium mean?

Webster and Collins seem to have the same idea for the word.

I hear it is about something or someone being completely wild!

I hear it is about being loud or noisy!

I hear it is an element of confusion or guess it- Pandemonium…. Here! Here!

I hear it is about confusion or disorder!

I hear it is Uproar

I hear it is about Chaos!

I hear the noise after a goal scored!

How do we get Pandemonium to get into play?

Think about Manchester united scoring a goal against Liverpool, Arsenal, Chelsea or against the other noisy neighbours, at Old Trafford.

Maybe it happened in 1966 England during the world cup.

Maybe a crazy celebratory night out with true mates

Yes, Pandemonium comes dressed in different attire, I have never heard of a word with that many different meanings.

Yet it all means the same!

But there you have it, Pandemonium, is a state of being with vast meanings!

## Passion

Open your eyes dear brother
Open your eyes dear sister
Open up to your inner desires
Open up to your commitments
Open up to your needs
Open up your inner continuum
Open up to love
Open up my dear friend

What is your desire buddy?
What are you going to do to achieve that desire?
What need does rock your boat?
What input are you making toward it?
What amount of energy do you need?
What brother, what?
What effort, what energy?

How much input have you made?
How much are you willing to live through?
How much are you willing to sacrifice?
How much of the maze can you go through?
How much income are you willing to sacrifice?

How much are you going to forego?

How much or how badly do you really want it?

How much? How much? How much?

Live it as a madman

Fight for it like a Viking

Jump for it like a horse

Keep moving my friend

Run, walk, crawl if need be brother

Yes, keep moving forward to achieve it

Put all your energy, love and strength into it

Go through the labyrinth

Yes my friend, live and love with passion

For it's the passionate that will concur this world

## People

They hate each other for no reason

They fight useless wars with nothing to gain from it

They kill each other with impunity

They revel in evil and vilify the righteous

They have fought two world wars, killing each other in millions in the process

Think of the atomic bombs in Hiroshima and Nagasaki

Remember 911, with thousands killed due to hate?

Reason, aiming to end up with 70 virgins in paradise if they commit suicide?

How great it could be having those virgins here and now without killing anybody or waiting to die.

The powerful Nuclear weapons that could annihilate millions in minutes

Mankind, mankind, what's wrong with you Mankind?

Some assemble bombs in suburban flats and end innocent lives

Think about 7/7 in London

The sad and bad news attracts myriads, while life-enhancing and positive news is ignored

The media that is supposed to inform thrives on negativity

Some kill each other for love. Imagine?

Governments attack each other; think Vietnam, Iraq, Afghanistan, or Libya

Priests prey on kids and nuns even with claims of celibacy

They hate each other because of their differing skin colours

Talk of the environment, The Amazon Forest being encroached upon,

The icecaps melting because of mankind's activities

Too much carbon monoxide being released in the atmosphere

Yes, as a Black man, I could talk about slave trade

The Whiteman enslaving the Blackman, But who sold those slaves to the Whiteman,

I can tell you!! The Black Man himself did!!!

Some people get hurt in the name of comedy

Weaponry and defence budgets soar higher while kids go hungry around the world and millions have no roof over their heads

Elitism has replaced traditional values

The you are either with them or with us mentality doesn't seem to stop

Trying to suppress each other is the order of the day

Yes allow me rant brother, allow me Rant

What is wrong with you Mankind?

African strongmen killing their populace while the world watches,

Remember the Rwandan Genocide?

The apartheid regime in South Africa

Why is suppression and oppression the order of the day?

Aggression is praised for strength while empathy and kindness are judged as weakness

The rich get richer while the poor get poorer

Suspicion towards each other is paramount

Can you imagine the top 10% own almost all of the world's wealth?

While kids around the world, are dying of malnutrition and preventable diseases.

Ganging up and gang culture is the order of the day.

Lust and misogyny are confused for love

The us against them mentality is taking root all the time

Unity is suppressed for personal gain instead of love and kindness

Yes my dear, something is wrong with Mankind

What is wrong can be beyond comprehension

However my brother, every cloud has a silver lining,

And there is always a light at the end of the tunnel

And I truly believe in the possibility of human kindness

For with that, we can understand what is wrong with people and maybe, in the end, find the solution for these evils

What is wrong with people?

That is a question worth studying and maybe, maybe in the end, we shall prevail if we get the answer

To this ever-challenging question

What is wrong with people??

## Pucker

It's all about how genuine one is.

It's about sincerity

It might be ancient Anglo-Saxon or Hindu in nature, but it still stands upright in the modern day.

Before kissing that special someone, pucker your lips. I am told it makes the kiss sweeter, but don't take my words or it.

It's about reliability and your weight in character

In the military, it's about the stress and adrenaline rush in the middle of combat.

It is the tightened knots and strength into small folds

In the end, you might need to be Hindu to know more about those goblins.

How tightened is your face and how is that relevant to the current narrative?

For a baby, it is just about when she or he wants to cry.

Puckering comes in different nips and bounds

It could be coarsening, creasing, folding, smoothening or straightening

But in the end, puckering is relevant in different circumstances.

## Repentance

John the Baptist had it in mind

For he knew the lord's kingdom was at hand

All sinners have to do it to be free

For survival, one has to do it

One wonders, how relevant is this?

To be forgiven, one has to do it

The dreams are innumerable

For just do it with plenty at heart

Forgive and you shall be forgiven

Turn away from your evil ways

For then, you shall be forgiven

Yes my brother and sister, for that matter,

turn away from your evil ways

Did you hate them for who they are?

Turn back from your evil ways

Did you cheat them for your progress?

Turn back from your evil ways

Did you hurt their feelings both intentionally and unintentionally?

Turn back from your evil ways

Did you think evil thoughts?

Turn back from your evil ways

Did you shutter their dreams intentionally?

Turn back from your evil ways

Did you rob them of their dignity?

Turn back from your evil ways

Do you hate for no reason?

Turn back from your evil ways

Look here my friend

Turn back from your evil ways

For selling your soul is death doubled

Be pure at heart and the best will come

Love with passion and diligence,

Use your intuition

Treat each other with empathy and evil will not prevail

Hear me dear friend, as John said

Repent for the kingdom of heaven is at hand

Repent, Repent, Repent

## Seeing is Believing?

Tell me your friends, and I will tell you who you are

For the birds of the same feathers flock together

Biblically saying, blessed are those who believe without seeing.

But who amongst us believes so?

Open my heart, dear Alpha and Omega,

For I would love to completely believe you are lord without necessarily seeing

For I know, you are Mighty Jehovah Jayila

Open my heart in the only way You can, for it is through your power that I will, and we shall be empowered

Teach me to believe mighty one, king of Zion

For I truly want to believe without seeing

Guide us, oh Jehovah, for it's through your touch that we can truly feel

Show us your power good lord for we truly need to believe

Open our eyes dear father, for it is only through you and your power that we can truly believe

Yes it's through you we can truly believe without seeing

Show us your love and mercy for its through your deeds that we shall learn to truly believe

Just like you helped the 12 become fishers of men and not fishers of fish

Just like you performed miracles in Canaan and Galleria, perform miracles in us so we can truly believe

I am not saying we shall only believe after seeing your miracles, but your works are all inspiring and duly enduring forever

Just open our eyes to see your miracles father of the universe

Just like you fed the 5000 with only five fish and two loaves of bread?

Just like you helped Simon Peter walk on water, resurrected Lazarus from the dead, helped the leper get up stand up and walk, Turned water into wine, even rising from the dead

Show us Lord God, Show us the right way for your people need to learn to believe

Empower us too so we can empower others

For its through believing in you that we shall be believed

Show me the way just like you did, through your miracles

I am not hoping to play magician mighty one, I just would love to be your child

For I would love to be better to make your people better

For I would love to be empowered in order to empower your people

How much more do I need to ask dear father?

For you know all I need even before I personally know it,

For heavy are the shoulders that wear this ever-precarious crown

If I am your choice dear one show me even if I sometimes warn in faith

For I truly want to whole heartedly believe in you without even seeing

It is indeed through only you that I can truly believe without seeing

For it is indeed through you that the masses can learn to believe

Let us learn to believe without seeing father of the fatherless

For it is through faith that we can truly be saved dear one.

Father of the fatherless El- Shadia

For at the end of the day, like you said in your big book, blessed are those who believe without seeing

For if you have faith and no doubt you can move mountains

For if you believe you can achieve whatever you ask for in prayer, as said in Mathew 21.

It's upon us, your servants, that have to believe even without seeing

For above is a prayer from your servant who would truly love to believe even without seeing

## Success

Success comes dressed in different attire

To one, it is a glass half-empty; to others, it is one half-full

To some success is about how much one has in his bank account

To others, it is about peace of mind

To one individual, success is determined by how happy one is

To others, it's about how much one can give.

To others, it's about things one possesses, the car, Jet, Yacht, bike, helicopter and maybe a big beautiful house on a beautiful Island

Maybe, it's about understanding yourself worth. After all, that too is progress to many

Success can be about the relationships one has. To some success is about that intimate connection with that special person or those special people in life.

Maybe it is about achieving that goal. An academic degree, or diploma, a master's degree or a PHD

Life achievements, like getting married, your first child, learning how to drive, your first car, first job, wedding anniversary, can all be considered success to some.

Some say it is about how long one lives, but to some it is about how one lives.

To most, success is not because of absence of problems, but just being well-equipped to solve those problems.

It's about being faithful with less so you can open up space to be blessed with more.

To a young man growing up in the African Savannas, success was about academic achievements, scoring a goal in a football game, which quickly metamorphosed to mundane stuff like having electricity and running water in the house.

Leaving the countryside for the city as a teenager was success too, but again success is about being hungry for more. Being popular amongst one's peers are successes to some.

Success is about little wins, a proper meal in your belly, a roof over one's head, friends, a lovely coffee in the morning, putting a smile on one's face, a cuddle from someone you like, seeing a smiley face, listening to your favourite tune on the radio, hanging out with friends and family, that cold beer on a Friday evening, a walk in the park or along the canal and maybe a lovely cold ice cream on a hot summer day.

Or maybe being able to buy a round of drinks for you and your friends without feeling the pinch

For one loses when he conquers man, but succeeds when he conquers his own fears, maybe, in the end, success is about conquering the said fears and heading for the stars

There might be no blue print to success, for success is different from individual to individual

Success is about paying the price in order to achieve that promise you crave for in your heart of hearts

In the end, success is about getting better for things to get better

It is about learning, growing and changing

In a nutshell, success is about being wiser, stronger and better

But in the end, success is about feeling the fear and doing it anyway in order to achieve one's goals

You might not score a winning goal in a football game, you might not dunk a three-pointer to win by a point or two in a basketball game, you might not run a marathon, you may not have landed that dream job, you may not have made that inspiring speech

But it the end success is relevant, determine your own individual success for success is an individual thing.

## Transition

It's the time in between

The feeling is euphoria probably ecstatic

However, he wonders

Are they snooping on him, or is it the diagnosis?

What could he do to get into the frame of mind?

Gone on for years it has, relenting they do not seem to.

This begs the question, why him?

Do they love or loath him?

Why do they go round in circles without telling?

What do they want of him?

Look Stranger!!

For the truth is in plain sight.

Just be clear and ask for what you want.

For they say seek and you shall find,

Ask, and it shall be given to you.

Is he their prisoner, or are they his hostages?

How will this end? Will it end well?

What is that well?

Why him? What is their secret? Or is it his secret?

Now friend look.

If I am part of the problem, I can be part of the solution.

Or so the adage goes.

Let us address the elephant in the room.

Let's open up, for what they are hiding is in plain sight, peacock style.

Let us talk desires my friend, what is your desire?

Can I help you achieve it?

What does it take to achieve our desires, everything. Right?

Who do I have to kill?

OK friend, It won't get to that.

Tell me... Do you want me for a friend? If so please tell.

Do you want me gone?

Or maybe you are challenging me to be the best I can be?

Or are you trying to suppress me?

Is it the ever-talked-about transition?

Why are they snooping around him?

Why so? Why so when he is here and can talk?

Are we transitioning towards a better world?

Or are we transitioning towards demise?

Do we have an end in sight? Or are we transitioning towards infinity?

For it is a lovely English word, Transition!!

Transition

Transition

## Transition

For this transition should be towards bigger and better

For if it's not for this, then all our efforts over the years have been futile.

Let's transition towards being our inner Gods.

For it is then that our transition will be worthwhile

There, here we go......

Let's transition before we are all left behind.

## Truth

Tell the emperor that he is naked
Address the elephant in the room
Say it even if it hurts
Reveal it even if it embarrasses
Showcase it even if it is frowned upon
Deliver it even if it angers them
Stand for it even if you stand alone
Be for it, even if they all desert you
Love it, for it is honourable
Go for it even though the majority deny it
Secure it, for it will save the world
Desire it for its passion prevails
Do not lose its track, for it prevails

Encourage your own to stand for it
Do not sweep it under the carpet
Let it shine bright, do not cover its flames
Let it inspire the masses
Let it be for your everyday
Saying it saves time, energy and other resources
Saying it could save the world
Standing for it as it is virtuous

All said and done, Stand for and say the truth

For the truth will absolve you

Or maybe it could save the universe

Let the truth be told, For the proof of the pudding is in the eating

**Unity**

Together as one we come up
Black brown or white we are
Yeah, true Rainbow. All spectrum
Forward as a team, we move
Onwards and upwards we go
Together at the centre of the universe
To go fast you can, to go far go together
What brings us together is way bigger
Stronger than what separates us.

It could be a platoon of soldiers
It could be a gang of youths
It could be a team bonding session
It could be Romeo and Juliet
It could be that true love
It could be that love that conquers all
It could be petting teenagers under a tree
It could be political allies
It could be a football team
It could be nations with similar interests
It could be a group with similar interest yeah. Trade Union style

You may have similar destinations

You may have similar goals and aspirations

You may need to move from A to B.

You may share a deep secret

You may have similar interests

You may be a family in need

You may be playing on the same team

You may together have a battle or war to fight

You may be under one leader

For we are in this together

For together the teeth crack the bone

For it is our beliefs that bind us

For it is our dearest that are familiar

For it is our dearest that are similar

For you reach out for me, and I reach out for you

For it is our empathy that matters

For it takes a village to raise a child

For we are different colours one people

For it could be under a religious umbrella

For it could be humankind or spiritual beings

For we could be fighting for the same cause

For it could be through music prose or poetry

For United we stand divided we fall

For it is a collective responsibility

For it is about serving one another

For we can unite and prosper together or die together as fools.

That is Unity in a nutshell.

## Universal Quest

It’s a Universal quest
One that you are for
The one you should be for
The journey is to the top
Yes, to the top
Top of the tree
Top of the races
Top of beings

It is a universal quest
For me and you
For the two of us
To go hand in hand
Arm in arm
The journey just started
Where to, nobody knows
Where from misunderstood.

Come Ye My friend
Come to me my friend
Come we trek
Yes trek hand in hand

Step by step

Inch by inch

Come Ye my friend

For we need each other

I need what you have

And I have what you need

For you are special

Yes special, exalted and all

Yes it is

It is a universal quest

For me and you

## Veil

Thinly embroiled in our being, nature takes charge

It could be an attire for nuns

It could be an attire for Islamic leaning ladies

For we are kept from the outside world with this attire

For concealed underneath this is an enigma.

Underneath this garment is what we desire to see

For when uncovered we find more

For when covered we are concealed

We find in-depth what was previously protected within

Think,

Brides love this, for it's on this their special day that they are concealed

For mankind is thinly veiled in kindness

But underneath, lies the devil's incarnate

What happens in Vegas stays in Vegas

For we could keep it all underneath

Concealment can be mystery sometimes

Obscure, blurred, half-light, Web, curtain, military camouflage. It is all in

Drape, enfold, disguise, mantle, shield are all in the word

Winter comes underneath this. Rain or Snow

Different folks different strokes

Different cultures have taboos and totems to keep themselves in check

The moon and darkness are embroiled in the night

Women have mastered this art

For through their smiles and sweetness they keep their feeling in check

Flirts use it to hide their shyness

Some hide their ways in humour, sarcasm and banter

Her aurora hides that sable covering

For all said and done veil stands for much more than covering

For it is through this veil that nature is kept under wrap

For it is through this veil that nature keeps its ugliness or sweetness all in one bound

For that veil could protect you more than you thought it could in your wildest dreams.

**Wassailing**

Let us go my friend

Let's pay a visit to the orchard

Maybe it is a smell of the flowers

Let that smell dive into your nose

Sweet sorrow isn't it?

And the aroma, delicious as cake

So that aroma hits one's nose

Let us go wassailing, for it is then that we shall admire the beauty of nature

Let us go wassailing for when we get there things will stand still

Let us go wassailing for it is then that we shall connect with nature

Maybe along the way we shall find some honey delicious and sweet

Sweet sorrow like being in love

Let's go for it is then we shall harness the beauty of this habitat planet earth

Let us make wassailing part of who we are

Demonic it might be but again its part of life

After all, the proof of the pudding is in the eating

Let us go wassailing for after all winter will be gone soon

**We are at War**

We are at war

We need to break them

Break these Glass ceilings

It has been done before

So it can be done again

The rule of Law

Magna carter

Limited Wars

Women Emancipation

Single-sex Marriages

Interracial Marriages

Cross generation relationships

As broken and all-changing

The Glass ceiling has

Yes has been broken

Disability, not inability

Age meaningless

Gender Meaningless

Colour blindness and all.

Together we shall

Break these glass ceilings.

Aluta Continua

## Wearing a Hat

Is it a black man's hat or a white man's hat?

Whose hat should I wear?

Who determines whose hat it is?

What makes you think it's your hat?

Is it your hat or my hat that you are wearing?

Now friend, think

Now friend, think

Now friend, think

I said Now friend, think

Is it a Magician's Hat?

Is it that little Hut housing the Thatcher?

Is it that military Hat the Beret?

Is it the other Heart that pumps blood through the ventricles

Is it the hurt that comes with pain?

Is it the other hurt that comes with passion?

How passionate are you, dear brother?

Is it the one worn by the big bearded Whiteman at Christmas?

Is it really?

Is it Santa's hat?

Is it the boys' brigades or a Boy Scouts'

Is it the girl guide or Cab Scout's hat?

If I wore my journalism hat, would I fit in?
If I wore my Marital Arts hat, would I win?
If I wore my salesman hat, would I close?
If I wore my Blackman's hat, would I get hurt?
If I wore my Whiteman's hat, would they hate me?
If I wore my Casanova's hat, would the girl yearn for me?
If I wore my commander's hat, would they follow me?
If I wore my British Hat, would I seem imperialistic?
Is imperialistic an English word?
If I wore my gypsy's hat, would I be scorned?
If I wore my Jester's hat would they love me?
If I wore my lover's hat, would they love me back?
Yes my dear, wear your hat, wear it proud!
For your hat is your brand
Go on, go wear your best Hat
Wear it proud wear it right

## What Can I Do For You?

What can I do for you my friend
How can I do it my friend?
Where can I go my friend?
Yes, my friend.
How can I serve you?
For you are dear to me.
My friend
Yes you
You my friend
Can I take your hand?
Can you take my hand?
And where shall we go?
Where to my friend?
But I know for sure
We shall get there
Yes
We shall get there my friend
To Infinity and Beyond.

## Wind

There it is, blowing onto my face

The breeze phenomenon

The air beautiful and gentle

The feeling of ecstasy, the state of mind ecstatic

In his childlike mind, the thought wondered to the gaseous strings

Yeah the smelly one.

Made better by boiled eggs and baked beans

Did I say better?

My long nose taking it all in. Dear me. Not into my lungs

The direction, varying from side to side. North, South, East and West.

Mind wonders about strength, hurricane, cyclone, tornado and all. The eye of the storm.

The waves at sea, the slides on the Mountains, the force

Strong and peculiar!

We cannot change it but we can adjust the sail

As we age, the stronger it is.

As it sweeps over the corn field, nature laughs in the sunshine

For we can hear it whisper though incomprehensible.

The mundane feeling of the air on your face

Reminds one for the wind and air is real and one indeed lives

For again and again, it shows us how close we are to the edge.

For if you want to know its strength, sail in its opposition.

That is for real, let's sail through, for through it all we shall know

Or probably sit, walk run or lie on a beach, you indeed will know

Wind has power that we cannot comprehend.

Wind has no equal!

## Window into the World

It is keeping your eyes peeled

It's about keeping your ears to the ground

Could it be through the media?

For the fourth estate does it better

Some dream to be part of

Others are part of the dream

Fame and fortune may come with it

It is a personal view from one's vantage point

It is in the eyes of the beholder like beauty

My view is not necessarily your view

My vantage point and your vantage point are dissimilar

Love it or loath it, it's part of who we are

Our ancestors did it over the campfire

The wireless eased it

The print harnessed it

Video killed the radio star

Then the internet took hold

Now we are at it, rolling in the deep

For it is part of who we are

Break the news or live in the limelight

For it could be you on the six O'clock news

Embrace it, be part of the story

For it is then that we are aligning with our true nature

That is my view in the window into the world

## Woodlands

Ever walked in the woods?

They say it is quiet and lonely but can be exciting and homely

Walking alone in the woods is a nightmare to some and bliss to others

Remembering my early morning milk run before school as a kid

The dark woods close to home remind me of how scared I was following stories of wild animals and ghosts in the woods

Fast forward to my most recent walk in the woods and comparing the two I am amazed how life really changes

The current walk in the woods is more therapeutical than fear inducing

The serene and settled majesty of woodland scenery comes in nips and bounds

The noble inclination cannot escape mention

The charm, and the Majesty of some woodland's nooks and crannies can be breath-taking

Walking or running in the woodlands helps one connect with Mother Nature, nothing connects one to mother nature more than that long walk or run in the woods

Woodlands create that insatiable appetite to connect with nature and nurture

Maybe it is the aura, the deep silence, the peace and solitude, of the overburdened mind, the tranquillity

Nothing else creates an air of awry, beyond man's affinity than woodlands, trees and forests

The swirling, waving, and tossing of branches, maybe it is because they were God's temples first

The purifying air, the fresh breeze, for life on earth is inconceivable without trees for they are our most intimate contact with nature

Go into the woods to lose yourself and find your soul for it's in the woodlands that you will find that solace.

They say Nature and spirituality come hand in glove for being in the woods is a beautiful thing

I wish I had learnt that as a kid when running through the woods scared of wild animals that probably never existed in the woods near my home

Connect with the woods for then you will have connected with nature at its purest

## You Reap What You Sow

You reap what you sow
Get Lemon make Lemonade
Love Roses and you will get!
You will get the Blisters too
Take the journey and destination beacons
Leap and you will reach
Yes, reach the heights
Soar like an Eagle
Reach for the stars
Or maybe then you will
Yes! You will get to the top
For the dream is real
Start the journey and visualise
The destination visualise
For we are all on the journey
Goodness knows when we shall
Shall ever get there. For
When we get there
Yes, Me and you!
Shall breathe fresh and sigh
Do sow with pleasure
Sow and you will reap much more

Word!

Printed in Great Britain
by Amazon

59464164R00079